History's Hotshots

NINJAS!
Skilled and Stealthy Secret Agents

Kelly Doudna

Checkerboard Library

An Imprint of Abdo Publishing
abdopublishing.com

abdopublishing.com

Published by Abdo Publishing, a division of ABDO, PO Box 398166, Minneapolis, Minnesota 55439.
Copyright © 2018 by Abdo Consulting Group, Inc. International copyrights reserved in all countries.
No part of this book may be reproduced in any form without written permission from the publisher.
Checkerboard Library™ is a trademark and logo of Abdo Publishing.

Printed in the United States of America, North Mankato, Minnesota
102017
012018

THIS BOOK CONTAINS
RECYCLED MATERIALS

Design: Kelly Doudna, Mighty Media, Inc.
Production: Mighty Media, Inc.
Editor: Rebecca Felix
Design Elements: Shutterstock
Cover Photograph: Shutterstock
Interior Photographs: Alamy, pp. 6, 15; iStockphoto, pp. 4-5; Kazuhiro Nogi/AFP/Getty Images, p. 24;
Library of Congress, pp. 8 (top), 9, 17; Mighty Media, Inc., p. 7; Shutterstock, pp. 1, 7, 8 (bottom),
25 (left), 25 (right), 29; Toshifumi Kitamuta/AFP/Getty Images, p. 27; Wikimedia Commons, pp. 8
(middle), 10, 11, 13, 18, 19, 21, 23

Publisher's Cataloging-in-Publication Data

Names: Doudna, Kelly, author.
Title: Ninjas! skilled and stealthy secret agents / by Kelly Doudna.
Other titles: Skilled and stealthy secret agents
Description: Minneapolis, Minnesota : Abdo Publishing, 2018. | Series: History's hotshots |
    Includes online resources and index.
Identifiers: LCCN 2017944054 | ISBN 9781532112720 (lib.bdg.) | ISBN 9781532150449 (ebook)
Subjects: LCSH: Ninja--Juvenile literature. | Ninjutsu--Juvenile literature. |
    Japan--History, Military--To 1868--Juvenile literature. | Japan--Juvenile literature.
Classification: DDC 355.548--dc23
LC record available at https://lccn.loc.gov/2017944054

Contents

SILENT
and
DEADLY

You lead a quiet daily life as a farmer, aiming to go unnoticed. You're an expert at veiling yourself among people. But you also have a secret job few know about. You wait for instructions for your next mission. The assignment might come from the head of a strong, regional family. **Samurai** or a daimyo may also hire you to help carry out an attack against a competing warlord.

You receive an attack mission from a samurai family, and you set out at once. You move soundlessly through the mountain forest, tracking your target. You stay still as a rock to hide from your enemy. You enter the icy water of a cold, spring-fed stream without **flinching**. These mountains are your home. And you have learned to blend in with their surroundings so well that you're nearly invisible.

Unlike the samurai who hired you, you are not bound by honor and ceremony. You know many **devious** methods to help you complete your mission. You are a master at carrying out calculated attacks while hiding in plain sight. The art of deception is your way of life. You are one of history's most effective warriors. You are a ninja!

CHAPTER 1

Hazy History

Ninjas have existed in popular **culture** for hundreds of years. But many aspects of their history are hard to confirm. This is because ancient Japan has a strong history of **oral** tradition, and spoken stories often vary in detail. Additionally, a ninja's main function was to be secretive. So, there was little written about these warriors. Because of this, historians disagree on exactly how ninjas developed.

A major point historians argue over is how great an influence the Chinese were on ninja development. Ninjas are a Japanese

Ninjas first appeared in Japanese text in the 1300s war chronicle Taiheiki.

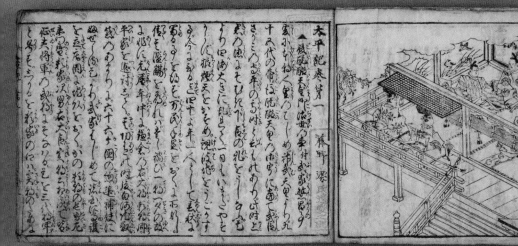

JAPANESE PROVINCES
OF THE HISTORIC NINJA

SEA OF JAPAN

KYOTO

KOKA

IGA

JAPAN

TOKYO

PACIFIC OCEAN

N
W   E
S

FEATURED AREA

warrior group with roots in the Iga and Koka **provinces**. However, many Asian **cultures** studied ancient Chinese texts. One important text was *The Art of War*. It was written by Chinese military **strategist** Sun Tzu in the 400s or 300s BCE.

The Art of War influenced military strategy throughout Asia. Many historians believe this text played a strong role in the formation of ninjas. The military skills ninjas use emerged in Japan between the 600s and 900s CE.

Historians believe Chinese **immigrants** also influenced ninja culture. When these immigrants began moving to Japan in the 1000s, they brought their war **tactics** and philosophies with them. Traces of these immigrant groups' influences are found in ninja culture.

Timeline

400s or 300s BCE *The Art of War* is written. It later influences Asian military **strategies** and ninja **culture**.

600s–900s CE The military skills ninjas use emerge in Japan.

1000s Chinese **immigrants** begin moving to Japan. These groups' ideas and practices can be found in ninja culture.

1477 The **Onin War** ends. The golden age of the ninjas begins.

1500s Oda Nobunaga attacks and defeats the ninjas of Koka and Iga.

1603–1867 During the Tokugawa shogunate, ninjas are used more for information gathering than attacks. The ninja golden age ends.

1967 The **inaccurate** image of ninjas in *You Only Live Twice* shapes modern mythology.

1984 Teenage **Mutant** Ninja Turtles **debut**. The cartoon characters increase ninjas' popularity around the world.

Prince Shotoku

The First Ninja?

No one is sure who the first ninja was. But stories suggest it may have been Otomono Sahito. Otomono served Japanese Crown Prince Shotoku. Shotoku lived from 574 to 622. Legends claim he employed Otomono as a spy. Shotoku shared battle techniques and philosophies of war with his employee. Historians believe Otomono may have been the first Japanese warrior to practice the arts of **stealth** and **infiltration**.

CHAPTER 2

Power Struggles

The golden age of the ninjas began in 1477 with the end of the **Onin War.** The Onin War had been fought to determine the heir to the Kyoto shogun, or military governor ruling Japan. Kyoto was the capital of Japan at the time. Its Imperial Court was the country's ruling government.

Warlords called daimyo ruled each **province**. These warlords fought one another for power. The war spread across all of Japan and ended without a clear victor. The daimyo remained in conflict with one another. A time known as the Warring States period began.

The provinces of Iga and Koka were near Kyoto. The citizens of these provinces were mountain dwellers. The areas did not have valuable farmland. So, feuding daimyo tended to leave the

Travel into the Iga province was difficult because of elevation and poor road conditions.

Samurai

Samurai and ninjas were contemporaries. Samurai was a social class that one was born into. A samurai's actions were closely tied to **rituals** and ceremonies that had been passed down through generations. These warriors promised to follow special codes and act with honor.

Ninja did not have these rules when completing missions. A samurai might hire a ninja to carry out tasks or missions thought dishonorable for a samurai to complete.

provinces alone during conflict. However, the clans of Iga and Koka fought amongst themselves for power.

Ninjas' abilities developed during these battles. The warriors used **unconventional** methods to defend the families that hired them. This included spying and using their expert knowledge of nature to hide and **ambush** targets.

Word of ninjas' special skills spread beyond Iga and Koka. Soon, daimyo and **samurai** families of the warring provinces wanted ninjas to work for them. Ninjas became an important weapon in the battles between these warlords.

Unification

Daimyo leaders hired ninjas for battles. But this working relationship was the most control warlords had over ninjas. Daimyo did not rule Iga or Koka. Instead, a **democratic** town council governed these **provinces**. Daimyo leaders in nearby provinces disapproved of this. One was Oda Nobunaga of Owari. Oda felt ninjas did not respect higher powers.

In the late 1500s, Oda attacked and defeated Koka's ninjas. He attacked the ninjas in Iga next. The ninjas who survived scattered, moving deeper into the mountains and to neighboring provinces.

Oda took power in other provinces and began to unify Japan. In 1582, one of his generals attacked Oda and forced him to kill himself. Then another of Oda's generals, Toyotomi Hideyoshi, overthrew this general and came to power himself.

Toyotomi continued Oda's work toward unification. In 1584, he was defeated by yet another of Oda's former generals, Tokugawa Ieyasu. Tokugawa completed the unification of Japan. The Tokugawa shogunate, or ruling military government, began in 1603.

Tokugawa Ieyasu (right) founded the last shogunate in Japan. Today, the country is ruled by governed officials, not the military.

Tokugawa did not share Oda's ideas about ninjas. He employed about two hundred ninjas who had scattered after their defeat by Oda. Under Tokugawa, these warriors' missions were more about gathering information and less about waging attacks. The Tokugawa shogunate lasted until 1867. Ninjas' services became less needed during this peaceful era. The ninja golden age came to an end.

Training and Knowledge

The mountainous landscapes of Iga and Koka greatly influenced ninja **culture.** The people living within these regions included *yamabushi*. Descriptions of *yamabushi* include "mountain hermit" and "warrior monk." *Yamabushi* believe their spirituality comes from living close to nature.

Yamabushi practice *shugendo*. This is using nature as a path to self-discovery. *Shugendo* is a spiritual process. But acquiring physical skills is a side effect. Practitioners train by putting themselves in extreme outdoor conditions. This includes being outside in harsh weather, walking through fire, and hanging over cliffs. The goal of these exercises is to overcome fear and absorb the powers of nature.

Historians believe *yamabushi* and *shugendo* practices influenced ninja training and knowledge. Remember, military techniques were passed down from Chinese **immigrants**, and Chinese texts were as well. The merging of these skills with *shugendo* practices made ninjas efficient warriors. They used any combination of **tactics** and tricks to overpower an enemy. This included **manipulating** people using beliefs about religion,

Yamabushi *still exist in Japan today. They center their lives on prayer and rituals.*

disguising themselves, and hiding. These **unconventional** means allowed ninjas to defeat enemy forces in great numbers.

Three Classes

There were three classes of ninjas. They were the *jonin*, *chunin*, and *genin*. Each class had different responsibilities related to missions. The *jonin* were the heads of strong families. They made important decisions about missions.

Chunin were the middlemen. A *chunin* received missions from a *jonin*. He then passed the information on to the *genin*. This was the lowest class of ninja. But *genin* were just as important as the other classes. These were the ninjas who carried out missions.

Genin trained from childhood. They had a warrior's knowledge and abilities. But these ninjas lived common everyday lives, often working as farmers and tradespeople. Because of these common day jobs, *genin* were able to blend in to enemy territories as workers. There, the ninjas kept a low profile until they were needed to execute a mission.

Ninjas of all classes were most often men. However, there were female ninjas too. They were known as *kunoichi*. These ninjas were members of the *genin* class.

Genin *could be promoted to* chunin *if they performed enough missions successfully.*

CHAPTER 6

Hiding among Many

Although different classes of ninjas received different training, all were taught the art of secrecy. Ninjas were known as *shinobi* in **medieval** Japan. Their techniques were referred to as *shinobi no jutsu*.

Ninjas were masters at disguising themselves as everyday workers in order to enter enemy territory unnoticed. As they performed tasks within enemy territory, ninjas also secretly gathered information.

A ninja priest may appear to pray for the dead on a battlefield while actually scouting nearby

Ninjas often disguised themselves as Japanese monks. These monks wore hats covering their heads, so ninjas dressed as them could easily conceal themselves.

Ninja is the Japanese pronunciation of the Chinese characters for "one who endures." Japanese also has its own character and word for ninja, *shinobi*. *Shinobi* was widely used in Japan in the past. Today, the Japanese use both terms, but *ninja* is most common outside of Japan.

"Ninja" written in Japanese kanji characters

enemy camps. A ninja merchant may be admitted into a castle to peddle his wares. However, his secret goal there was to spy on castle residents. Ninjas also posed as entertainers, story-tellers, and more.

Disguise was not a ninja's only skill among enemies. Ninjas were also experts at interacting with new people without raising suspicion. These warriors often gave the impression of being able to read the minds of their opponents. But ninjas were not mind readers. They were simply good at observing facial expressions, listening to tone of voice, and interpreting body language.

Natural Navigation

Ninjas were also skilled at going unnoticed in nature. They knew how to expertly blend in to their surroundings. They could also imitate its elements.

A ninja imitated a stone by being completely still and taking short breaths. He disappeared in lakes or streams using a bamboo pole to breathe from underwater. Ninjas wore black or navy in the forest at night. These colors made them hard to see among the dark trees.

Their familiarity with nature also served ninjas well when executing a mission. They predicted weather conditions by observing the color of the sky. This allowed ninjas to determine the most favorable time to strike at an enemy.

Ninjas also studied how local tides and currents change over the course of a day. They used these patterns to keep track of time. And they navigated by observing the positions of the moon and stars.

Hotshot Fact

Ninjas often wore shoes with soft, padded soles to help them walk around without making a sound.

Ninjas practiced tanuki-gakure, *the art of climbing a tree and blending in with its leaves and branches.*

CHAPTER 8

Secret Weapons

Ninjas were masters at turning everyday items into useful tools. They also turned these items into weapons. In the hands of a ninja, sticks, string, and even clothing became deadly to his or her enemy.

Some ninjas wore straw hats called *amigasa*. They pulled these hats over their faces to easily conceal their identities. Ninjas may have also hidden small weapons under these hats.

Kunoichi, or female ninjas, also made use of their head **apparel** during missions. They sharpened the ends of their ornamental hairpins. When poison was added to these sharpened tips, the hairpins became effective weapons.

Leather gloves became weapons when ninjas added a hook to the tip of each finger. These hooks could fend off a sword or scratch an enemy's face. Ninjas also added hooks to the ends of ropes. This

Hotshot Fact

Female ninjas, or *kunoichi*, were successful at entering enemy territories disguised as servants and dancers. Their missions were usually to gather information. But sometimes they were hired to kill.

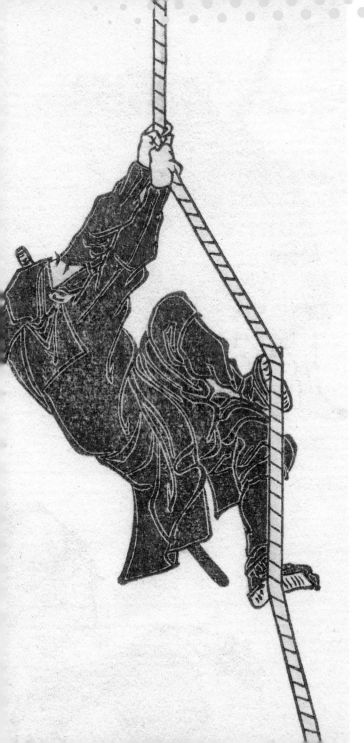

turned the ropes into *kaginawa*, or climbing tools.

Bamboo poles were especially useful to ninjas. A fan attached to one end turned a bamboo pole into an oar. A chain tied to one end transformed the pole into a weapon. A ninja held the pole and swung the chain in an attack. He could also use a bamboo pole to deliver poison darts.

Ninjas used ropes, hooks, and even collapsible bamboo ladders to infiltrate castles or other areas.

Water, Fire, and Metal

The way ninjas used certain everyday items was so clever that legends formed suggesting these warriors had supernatural powers! When crossing a waterway, a ninja would sometimes wear a bucket on each foot. The buckets kept him afloat as he stood upright in water. When the ninja moved his legs, it looked as though he were walking on water! Ninjas also balanced atop large, flat wooden circles that floated on the water's surface. This made it look as though the ninjas were able to float without a boat.

Water wasn't the only element ninjas mastered. They also knew many tricks that made it appear as though they had supernatural power over fire. These sly warriors were early adopters of **gunpowder**. During training, they learned more than 50 ways to use fire and explosions. One

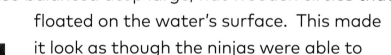

A ninja performer uses flame during a show at the Iga Ninja Museum in 2012.

HANDHELD JAPANESE WEAPONS

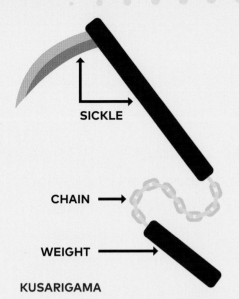

SICKLE

CHAIN →

WEIGHT →

KUSARIGAMA

A *kusarigama* was the combination of a sickle, chain, and weight. The weight would be thrown toward the enemy's weapon, causing the chain to wrap around and capture it. Then, the ninja could deliver a strike with the sickle.

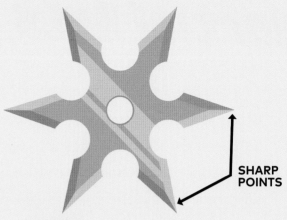

SHARP POINTS

SHURIKEN

A *shuriken* was a multi-pronged metal weapon. Its sharp points were used to cut or deliver poison. The *shuriken* is commonly known as a "throwing star." But historians disagree about how far or how accurately it could actually be thrown.

was using a small explosion to create a smokescreen. A ninja would quickly exit behind this veil of smoke. An enemy would think the ninja had disappeared into thin air!

Ninjas learned to make flares, rockets, and weatherproof torches. They obtained deadly tools as well. This included poisonous gas and grenades. Ninjas also used handheld Japanese weapons called *kusarigama* and *shuriken*.

CHAPTER 10

Martial Arts

The number and importance of ninjas **declined** in the 1600s. But their skills have been passed on to many generations and **cultures** throughout history. Ninjas' survival skills and **tactics** have collectively been known as ninjutsu. These practices continue today and are taught in modern martial arts schools.

Martial arts is the practice of combat and self-defense as sport. Several divisions of this sport focus on direct competition with an opponent. Today, this includes ninjutsu. However, many modern practitioners argue that ninjutsu today is too different from the classic practice to be given this title. Historic ninja ninjutsu practices involved approaching an opponent using **stealth** and **unconventional** skills. Today's ninjutsu practices focus more on direct combat and fighting.

Experts may not agree on whether true ninjutsu practices exist today. But skills similar to those of the historic ninja can still be found. Military special forces around the world train using stealth techniques similar to those ninjas used. These include the Army Rangers and Navy SEALs.

Modern ninjutsu practitioner Kazuki Ukita wears an interpretation of ninja apparel and poses at a ninja museum in Japan in 2002.

Modern Mythology

Modern mythology has greatly influenced ninjas' role in **culture.** However, historians feel these depictions are often **inaccurate** to historic ninjas. In Western cultures, modern ninja mythology is traced to the 1967 film *You Only Live Twice*.

In the film, secret agent James Bond trains with a school of ninjas. Unlike historic ninjas, these ninjas are less interested in martial arts. They are portrayed as more of a military unit specializing in surprise attacks.

Beginning in 1984, Teenage **Mutant** Ninja Turtles further influenced the way people thought of ninjas. These cartoon creatures **debuted** in a comic book that year. The turtles are trained in ninjutsu. They live underground until they are called upon to battle criminals, other mutants, and aliens.

The Teenage Mutant Ninja Turtles were an immediate hit. They were soon featured in films, TV shows, and toys. Their popularity spread ninjas' popularity around the world.

Cartoon turtles are just one example of ninja skills equaling supernatural powers in modern mythology. The idea of ninjas having these powers continued in later decades.

The Teenage Mutant Ninja Turtles have been featured in six films! The characters are also found on apparel and have become popular Halloween costumes.

Ninjas are often depicted in comics, TV shows, and films as being able to disappear, fly, crawl on ceilings, and more. While these skills are not true to the historic ninja, they reflect the fascination people have for these warriors. Modern **culture** remains amazed by the methods of the ninja!

Glossary

ambush – to conduct a surprise attack from a hidden position.

apparel – clothing.

culture – the customs, arts, and tools of a nation or a people at a certain time.

debut – to make a first appearance.

decline – to become inferior, weaker, or lower in amount.

democratic – related to a governmental system in which the people vote on how to run their country.

devious – misleading or not direct.

flinch – to draw back quickly and suddenly from pain or fear.

gunpowder – a dry, explosive substance used in firearms.

immigrant – a person who enters another country to live.

inaccurate – not precise or correct.

infiltrate – to enter a place secretly and without permission.

manipulate – to change something or influence someone's thoughts for one's own purpose.

medieval – related to the time period in Japan from 1185 CE to 1600 CE.

mutant – a living thing that is different from others of its kind because of a change in its genes.

Onin War – a civil war that took place in Japan from 1467 CE to 1477 CE.

oral – spoken instead of written.

province – a political division of a country.

ritual – a set form or order to a ceremony.

samurai – a Japanese warrior who lived in medieval times.

stealth – the act of performing in a secretive manner.

strategy – a careful plan or method. A person who makes this plan is a strategist.

tactic – a method of moving military forces in battle.

unconventional – unusual or not typical.

Online Resources

Booklinks
NONFICTION NETWORK
FREE! ONLINE NONFICTION RESOURCES

To learn more about ninjas, visit **abdobooklinks.com**. These links are routinely monitored and updated to provide the most current information available.

Index